Victorian and Edwardian

Crime and Punishment

from old photographs

A City of London policeman controlling traffic in 1873

Victorian and Edwardian

Crime and Punishment

from old photographs

Introduction and Commentaries by

RICHARD WHITMORE

B.T. BATSFORD LTD
LONDON

First published 1978
Copyright Richard Whitmore 1978

Filmset by Servis Filmsetting Ltd, Manchester
Printed in Great Britain by
The Anchor Press Limited,
Tiptree, Essex
for the publishers B.T. Batsford Ltd,
4 Fitzhardinge Street, London W1H 0AH

ISBN 0 7134 0348 9

By the same author

OF UNCOMMON INTEREST
True stories and photographs
of ordinary people and extraordinary events
in Victorian and Edwardian times

VICTORIAN AND EDWARDIAN HERTFORDSHIRE
from old photographs

Contents

Acknowledgements

Illustration number 32 is from the Royal Library at Windsor Castle and is reproduced by gracious permission of H.M. The Queen.

The Author and Publishers would also like to thank the following for permission to reproduce photographs: Avon and Somerset Police (26, 31, 81, 85, 138, 147); The Police College Library, Bramshill House Hampshire (18, 23, 37, 117); Cambridgeshire Constabulary (65–67); Central Press Photos Ltd (60); Chelmsford and Essex Museum (128); The Chief Constable of Cheshire (38, 109); Devon and Cornwall Constabulary (2, 24, 83, 108, 120, 144, 146); Richard Ford (107); John Girvan (79); City Museum and Art Gallery, Gloucester (3, 47, 52, 53, 57, 59, 63, 114); Mr Bryn Parry, County Archivist, Gwynedd County Council (12, 137); Hertfordshire Constabulary (1, 30, 42–46, 48–51, 54, 55, 61, 62, 75, 86–97, 110, 112, 113, 115, 116); The Home Office Prison Department (58, 64); Lincolnshire Police (5–7, 11); Ralph B. Lindley (25, 122); City of London Police (16, 29, 33, 70, 72); Greater Manchester Police (28, 106, 118, 139); Manchester Central Art Gallery (119); City of Manchester Cultural Services, Local History Library (4, 21, 36, 40, 73, 136); The Commissioner of Police, New Scotland Yard (14, 15, 76, 80, 98–101, 103, 130, 131, 143); Newport Public Library (126); The Local Studies Centre, Old Central Library North Shields (145); Portsmouth City Museums (27); The Press Association Ltd (132, 133); Radio Times Hulton Picture Library (20, 69, 82, 102, 121, 123, 135); Don Rumbelow (129); South Tyneside Central Library, South Shields (105); Surrey Constabulary (10, 17, 77); Thames Division Police Museum (127); Harold White of White Crescent Press Ltd, Luton (141); North Yorkshire Police (19, 39, 41, 104, 111, 134); West Yorkshire Metropolitan Police (8, 140); The remaining photographs are from the Author's and Publishers' collections.

Introduction

The photographs in this collection concentrate broadly on two groups of people involved in the system of law and order during Victorian and Edwardian times. In the first, those employed to enforce that system – the old nightwatchman with his sword and rattle, the lone parish constable, the prison officers and the proud ranks of the country's first organised police forces. In the second group are those who for a variety of reasons chose to challenge the law – murderers, convicts, women pickpockets or simply erring motorists, social protesters and little children who were sent to prison because they stole in order to eat. Through these early photographic records from many parts of the country the book sets out to show something of the lives and working conditions of the police, of the crimes and problems that confronted them and of the treatment of the law-breakers they caught. The period (1845–1914) is a fascinating one which witnessed many important reforms and yet still retained attitudes and conditions considered primitive by modern standards. The pictures tell their own stories; this introduction is intended as a back-cloth against which to view them.

The Police

By 1845, when photography was still an infant 'art-science', the first comprehensive police force – The Metropolitan Police of London – was well-established and other local authorities had begun to realise that a large organised force covering a wide area could be far more efficient than leaving the hundreds of small communities to arrange their own security by appointing a solitary nightwatchman or parish constable. The Municipal Corporation Act of 1835 had set the ball rolling by giving the new boroughs power to set up and run their own police forces through a Watch Committee. This was followed four years later by the County Police Act – the 'permissive act' as it became known – which *allowed* local justices to establish a paid police force in their respective counties but did not *order* them to do so. The vague wording of this act, coupled with fierce opposition from many areas on the grounds of cost, resulted in only a small number of new forces being formed and another 17 years were to pass before the Government of the day decided more positive action was needed. They passed the County and Borough Police Act of 1856 – the 'obligatory act' – which *ordered* local justices and watch committees to each

1 Punishment in the stocks *c.*1855

set up a paid police force in their respective area forthwith. This time the legislation worked, Home Office Inspectors of Constabulary were appointed and the country had finally achieved a network of borough and county constabularies that lasts until the present day – though some lost their original identity when they were absorbed into other forces during the local government re-organisation of the 1970s.

The camera arrived in time to capture just a flavour of those important transitional days in the middle of the last century so that there are in existence a few records of original nightwatchmen and parish constables (17, 18, 19) and even of policemen super-vising – with apparent good humour all round – punishment of local miscreants in the stocks (1, 108). Far more plentiful are photographs taken to record ceremonial occasions marking the formation of a new force or the issue of a new uniform. Dress styles changed a number of times during the Victorian and Edwardian eras; they began with the tall top hat, flared tunic and duck trousers, carefully modelled on the navy uniform of the day so that the police would not be confused with the army when dealing with civil disturbances. In fact the uniforms of later years were modelled to a greater degree on army styles and in 1855 when the British Army changed to the French pattern of dress, the police followed suit. Then, in 1870, after the defeat of the French in the Franco–Prussian War, police helmets arrived on the scene clearly copied from the *Pickelhaube* – the spiked helmet worn by the victorious German Army. It was this change that set the style of the police helmet which, with some modifications, is still worn today.

The life of a Victorian policeman was a hard one; in the 1850s most young men who joined the ranks came from the labouring classes, encouraged by parents who saw the job as a rare oppor-tunity for secure employment. For wages of between 15s 0d and one guinea these young constables would work a seven-day week, walking up to 20 miles a day on foot patrols. Until 1870 rest days were almost unheard of and if a man was sick or took seven days' annual leave his pay was stopped. Only in the last ten years of the century did police working conditions begin to improve. A senior officer, too, would find himself involved in much more than simply 'keeping the peace', being put in charge of other public services that nowadays justify their own staff and departments. A good example was the Head Constable of Godalming, Surrey, who in 1880 was also Inspector of Nuisances, Inspector of Common Lodging Houses, Inspector of Explosives, Inspector under the Petroleum Act, Inspector under the Dairy and Cowsheds Act, Inspector under the Food and Drugs Act and Billet Master.

Probably the most memorable additional service performed by

the early police forces was fire-fighting (104, 105, 106, 107). For a long time towns depended on a Volunteer Fire Brigade, manned by residents and traders and financed by local goodwill and donations from insurance companies. However, as equipment became more sophisticated and therefore more expensive, many brigades were taken over by the local authority and when that happened they were put under the control of the police department. This dual role sometimes caused friction with the Home Office who felt that, while policemen were fighting fires, their area was deprived of proper protection against crime. Nevertheless, the system continued for a long time and many towns and cities ran a highly-efficient Police Fire Brigade right up until 1941 when the fire services were nationalised as a war-time emergency.

Prison and Punishment

By the mid-nineteenth century, inspired by the earlier campaigns of John Howard and Elizabeth Fry, Victorian society was beginning to put its prison system onto a uniform and more constructive footing; new prisons were built and new standards of discipline and training introduced by which it was hoped the convict would leave not simply 'punished' but reformed as well. It was the ending of transportation which forced the country to start thinking seriously about how to deal with its hardened criminals. As one British colony after another refused to remain a dumping ground for the thieves and murderers of the Mother Country, Parliament found itself under more and more pressure to introduce new accommodation for the hundreds of convicts which for so long they had been able conveniently to deport and forget. In 1864 penal servitude (punishment by hard work) was introduced as the alternative to transportation. More convict prisons were opened, among them Dartmoor (86–97). The convicts sent there knew they were in for a hard time but at least they were not without hope. For the new punishment system, while extremely tough, also offered incentives to learn a trade and to achieve promotion, privileges and even remission of sentence by earning marks – the number of marks to be earned depending on the severity of the sentence. By and large the men were engaged on 'public works' from which the community as a whole could benefit – stone quarrying, road building and the construction of quays and breakwaters for dockyards. There was even a period when prisoners more than earned their keep; in 1871 men at Portland, Portsmouth and Chatham prisons earned between them £149,000 while the total cost of running the same prisons that year was only £131,000. Wormwood Scrubs in West London – described in the 1890s as 'the model prison of England, if not the world' – was built entirely by convict labour and cost the country only £75 per cell unit, compared with

2 The St Columb Horse Bus being used to transport a prisoner to Bodmin gaol, Cornwall, in the 1880s

£500 per unit had the work been put out to private tender.

There was considerable debate over how the new prisons should be run. The main school of thought favoured the Separate System under which a prisoner spent his sentence in almost total solitary confinement, working, eating and sleeping alone in his cell with only an hour's exercise each day. The theory behind this was that, away from the bad influence of other criminals and left alone with his thoughts, a man could be 'softened up' over a period of months and then brainwashed by the staff and prison chaplain into thoughts of leading a better way of life. Unfortunately the system produced tragic side-effects. The loneliness drove some men to madness and suicide, forcing the authorities to modify their ideas so that men would spend only the first two or three months of their sentence in the 'solitary' cells. Other prisons adopted the Silent System under which prisoners were permitted to work and eat together but were forbidden to speak or look at each other. It was the task of the staff to enforce that silence by imposing a discipline based almost entirely upon fear – fear of being put to hard labour on machines which would now be classified as instruments of torture. Two of the most notorious of these were the treadwheel and the crank (3, 111, 112, 115).

The treadwheel was a large cylinder, some six feet in diameter, with rows of steps on the outside surface. As the prisoners stepped on it, the wheel began to turn under their weight and the men would have to start 'climbing' in order to stay in the same position. Each session, morning and afternoon, would last for three hours, the men having five minutes rest every 15 minutes. In this way they would climb about 9,000 feet each day – twice the height of Ben Nevis! Treadwheels at least served a small useful purpose in that the power they generated could be harnessed for such tasks as grinding corn, pumping water or operating a circular saw. The crank was completely demoralising in that it had no end product. Resembling the handle of a heavy mangle it was set at 12 lbs pressure, each turn of the handle being registered on a counter. The 'tasks' set on this nasty machine would range from 10,000 to 12,000 revolutions a day. It was not unusual for the stricter (or more sadistic) prison staff to make convicts earn their meals by performing, say, 2,000 revolutions before breakfast, another 5,000 before lunch and so on. A Royal Commission appointed in the 1870s to look into cruel punishments discovered one gaol at which a man had eaten only nine meals in 21 days because he had failed to complete the number of revolutions ordered by the staff. It was to prevent such maltreatment and to establish an acceptable uniform discipline throughout the country that the Prison Act of 1878 was passed. This took all prisons out of the hands of local authorities and brought them – like the convict prisons – under the control of the Home Office. Even so, it was another 20 years before excessive forms of hard labour and corporal punishment were abolished completely and at the turn of the century there were still 13 treadwheels installed in British prisons.

Improvements in the treatment of child offenders (64, 65, 66, 67) were also painfully slow arriving. Although it had been argued since the beginning of the nineteenth century that children should be kept separate from adults and although a system of juvenile reformatories had been established in the 1850s it was not until the 'Children's Charter' of 1908 that the separation was finally achieved. Between 1850 and 1900 the most common punishment given to children of both sexes was a short period of a month in prison with the *intention* that they should complete the rest of their sentence in a reformatory. However, through either accommodation problems or general laxity many youngsters spent the whole sentence in an adult prison and as late as 1894 a government inquiry disclosed that many children under 16 and some even under 12 were still being imprisoned among adults.

3 (*left*) Prisoners on the treadwheel at Gloucester gaol in the late 1890s

4 (*below*) Manchester City policemen with churchwarden pipes *c.*1850

Photography

The first Criminal Records files were started unofficially by a few prison governors as early as the 1850s, but it was in 1870 that the Prevention of Crimes Act made the photographing of prisoners compulsory. The following year more than 30,000 'rogues gallery' portraits poured into Scotland Yard and 375 arrests were made as a direct result of criminals being identified from their photographs. Apart from this official work, photographers were rarely allowed inside prison walls, which makes those scenes of routine prison life produced in this book the more unusual. They came from two main sources. The photographs of Gloucester gaol were taken at the turn of the century by John Rex Walter, a warder who was also a keen amateur photographer whose work is now preserved at the City Museum, Gloucester. The larger collection, depicting life at Wormwood Scrubs, Pentonville and on Dartmoor were taken in the 1890s by a London man, Mr W.H. Grove. They were used primarily to illustrate a lantern-slide lecture given to Victorian church groups and philanthropic societies by Mr R. Stubbings, who was on the staff of Wormwood Scrubs prison. It was a venture which required special Home Office permission and the lecture caused considerable interest at the time. The slide collection and Mr Stubbings' original lecture notes were donated to Hertfordshire Constabulary for safe-keeping some years ago. Mr Stubbings' lecture reflects the great pride felt by the latter-day Victorians in the reforms brought about during that era to improve the prisoners' lot . . . improvements which, for many, made prison a positive sanctuary from the appalling living conditions endured by so many thousands of the Victorian poor. On the day he was released from Pentonville one man summed up the situation in four words scratched on the wall of his cell – *In thin, out stout*.

Richard Whitmore,
Hitchin,
Herts.
1978

Photographing crimes and criminals
—the first steps

5 Three prisoners at Derby gaol *c.*1857. William Garbutt,
the deputy governor, was an enthusiastic amateur
photographer who, between 1857 and 1873 kept an
unofficial portrait album of many suspects and convicts
who came within his prison walls

6, 7 A husband-and-wife pickpocket team, Thomas and Louisa Parsons, photographed at Derby gaol in 1865 while they were serving a one-month sentence

8 A police 'wanted' notice of the kind published regularly by the old West Riding Constabulary at Wakefield, Yorkshire, in Victorian times. Until the development of screen photographic blocks at the turn of the century woodcut blocks were made from a photograph or sketch of the suspect

Police Reports

(ENTERED AT STATIONERS' HALL).   (TWENTYFIRST YEAR).

Published every **MONDAY, WEDNESDAY, & FRIDAY** Evening, for the information and use of the County and Borough Police of the West Riding of Yorkshire.

☞ All Notices for insertion in the POLICE REPORTS will be forwarded as soon after the Occurrence as circumstances will admit, addressed "PRINTING DEPARTMENT, WEST RIDING CONSTABULARY, WAKEFIELD." Reports received BEFORE THREE O'CLOCK IN THE AFTERNOON on days of Issue will appear; those received AFTER that hour will be shewn in next Reports. The Names and Descriptions of Persons known to have committed Crimes, Property Stolen &c., must be carefully and correctly given for the purpose of tracing them; and every Police Officer in expected to take it for granted, that the Persons wanted and Property described, are in his district, until he shall have made every enquiry, and satisfied himself that neither are on his Beat. The Officer forwarding particulars of offenders, whose names are known, and who are wanted, will affix his name and Rank as an authority. As every Issue contains new Occurrences, it is absolutely necessary that a copy of each be filed for further reference, writing off traced cases as the same occur. Officers and Sergeants in charge of Sections will circulate this Paper amongst their men as soon as practicable.

(No. 2995.)   MONDAY, FEBRUARY 13th, 1888.

POLICE NOTICE.

DESCRIPTION (AND PORTRAIT) OF

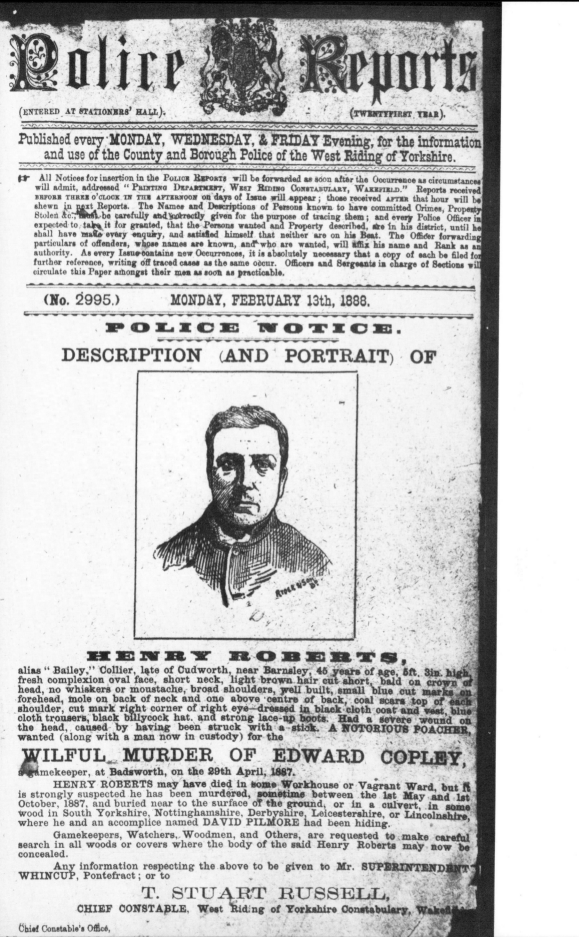

HENRY ROBERTS,

alias "Bailey," Collier, late of Cudworth, near Barnsley, 45 years of age, 5ft. 3in. high, fresh complexion oval face, short neck, light brown hair cut short, bald on crown of head, no whiskers or moustache, broad shoulders, well built, small blue cut marks on forehead, mole on back of neck and one above centre of back, coal scars top of each shoulder, cut mark right corner of right eye—dressed in black cloth coat and vest, blue cloth trousers, black billycock hat. and strong lace-up boots. Had a severe wound on the head, caused by having been struck with a stick. A NOTORIOUS POACHER, wanted (along with a man now in custody) for the

WILFUL MURDER OF EDWARD COPLEY,

a gamekeeper, at Badsworth, on the 29th April, 1887.

HENRY ROBERTS may have died in some Workhouse or Vagrant Ward, but it is strongly suspected he has been murdered, sometime between the 1st May and 1st October, 1887, and buried near to the surface of the ground, or in a culvert, in some wood in South Yorkshire, Nottinghamshire, Derbyshire, Leicestershire, or Lincolnshire, where he and an accomplice named DAVID PILMORE had been hiding.

Gamekeepers, Watchers, Woodmen, and Others, are requested to make careful search in all woods or covers where the body of the said Henry Roberts may now be concealed.

Any information respecting the above to be given to Mr. SUPERINTENDENT WHINCUP, Pontefract; or to

T. STUART RUSSELL,

CHIEF CONSTABLE, West Riding of Yorkshire Constabulary, Wakefield.

Chief Constable's Office,

No. 2. Mary Ann Travers
Clever street thief
26 old
5ft 2½ high
Brown eyes
Brown hair
Fresh Comp
3 mos G. Hall 14th Ap: 70
Dischd July 1870
Former convictions

No. 19. Ann Spencer
Shop thief
18 old
4ft 9. high
dark hair
grey eyes
fair comp
18mo: C.C.C. Nov: 1869.

No. 85. John Cox
Larceny
24 old
5ft 4. high
brown hair
grey eyes
fresh comp
12mo: C.C.C. July 1870

No. 94. Mary Jones
Street thief
32 old
5ft high
dark hair
hazel eyes
fresh comp
15mo: C.C.C. May 1870
other convictions

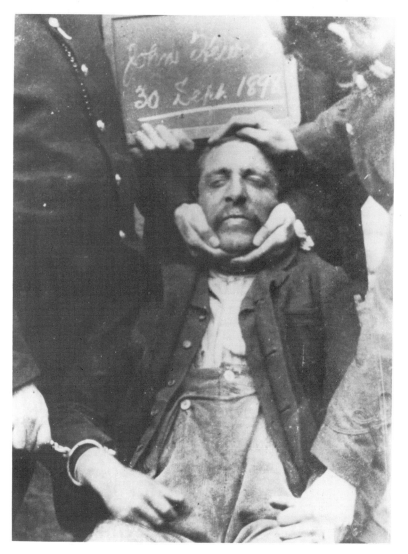

10 Some suspects objected violently
to being photographed – witness John
Hewett at Farnham Police Station,
Surrey, in 1898 who had to be
restrained by three burly policemen
and even then managed to keep his
eyes closed. The fairly long time-
exposure needed would have added
to the photographer's problems on
occasions such as this

9 A page from the first Criminal
Records File compiled by the City of
London Police from the 1860s

11 By the end of the nineteenth century the police had recognised the value of profile portraits to make identification easier. A popular method was to sit the prisoner in front of a set of mirrors and photograph him from behind, so obtaining several facial angles in one picture

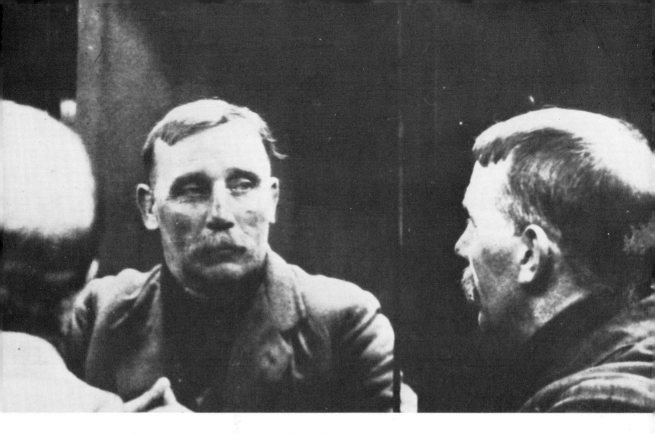

12   Pedlar Jane's love of the bottle and her subsequent court appearances in North Wales led to her being registered as 'a habitual drunkard'. At the turn of the century notices such as these were still circulated among drinking establishments throughout Britain

13   The Fox Twins, Albert Ebenezer and Ebenezer Albert (born 1857) were celebrated Hertfordshire poachers who between them collected 220 convictions for Game Law offences. They usually poached separately and escaped conviction many times when witnesses became confused over their identity. This ploy worked less frequently after the introduction of finger-printing for Criminal Record files during the Edwardian era

14 (*right*) The first photographic department at New Scotland Yard *c*.1905. By this time the police were beginning to use photography to record evidence at the scene of a crime

15 (*below*) Superintendent Frank Froest, executive head of the CID at New Scotland Yard in 1905

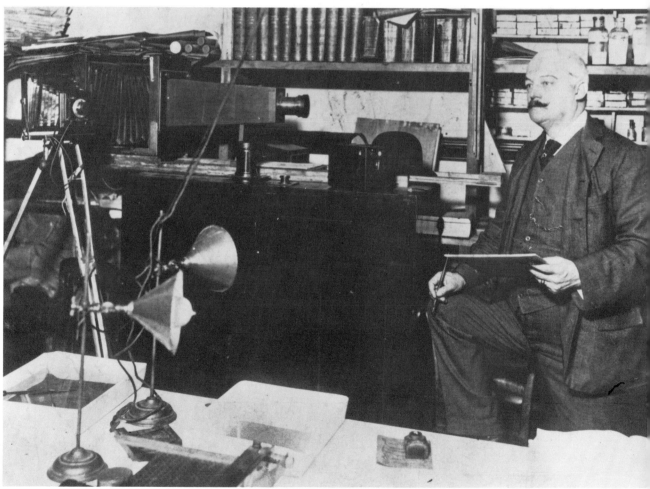

16   An East End murder victim of
the 1870s. Limited photographic
facilities meant corpses suffered the
indignity of being taken out into the
mortuary yard and propped against a
wall

Police portraits, groups and uniforms

17 Pc Carpenter – a photograph to record his appointment
as village constable at Clandon, Surrey, in 1857. The
average pay for a constable at this time was 18s 0d a week.
There was later an annual allowance of £1 14s 0d for boots

18 The last of the London nightwatchmen outside his box in Brixton Road and displaying the full range of weaponry and equipment carried by the 'charleys' on their parish rounds – lantern, truncheon, cutlass and alarm rattle. Photograph *c*.1870

19 (*above*) Thomas Newton, first
village constable of Middleton Tyas,
Yorkshire, *c*.1857. Pc Newton retired
from the North Riding Constabulary
in 1871

20 (*right*) Tom Smith, a well-known
London policeman, photographed by
Claudet in 1856. Claudet, a pioneer
French photographer, was one of the
first men to introduce daguerrotype
portraiture to England

21 (*right*) One of the earliest-known photographs of a police force showing men of the Manchester City Police outside Albert Street Station and reputedly taken in 1845–46

22 (*below*) Three Oxford policemen – Inspector Dixon, Chief Constable Head and Sergeant Miller in the courtyard of the old Town Hall which was demolished in 1892. Photograph *c*.1880

23 (*far right*) An early attempt to use photography to glamorise life in the Police Force – showing two men of Wokingham division, Berkshire, 'arresting' a suspect in a local photographic studio *c*.1860

24 (*left*) The working uniform of a superintendent in the Cornwall Constabulary in 1899

25 (*above*) Superintendent James Nimrod Race, chief of Liverpool Mounted Police, wearing the full ceremonial dress of 1898

26 The Chief Constable of Bristol, Henry Allbutt, with his superintendents at the turn of the century

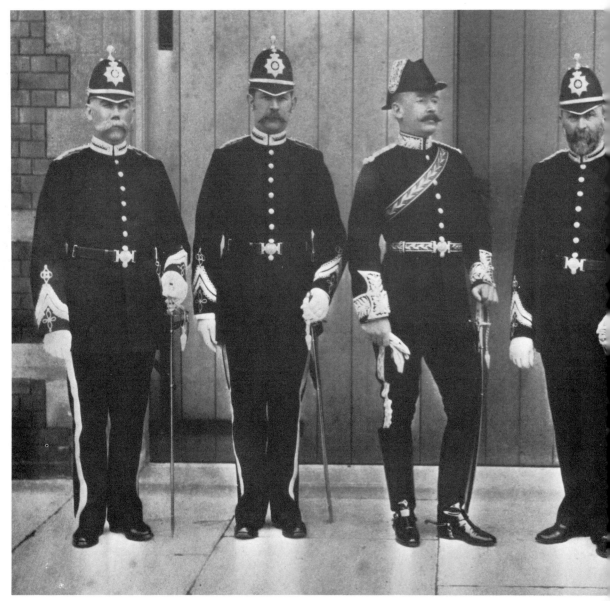

27   The Portsmouth Police Force
outside the old Landport Police
Station in 1865

28 (*left*) Detectives attached to the Rochdale division of the Greater Manchester Police in 1890

29 Sir James Fraser, Police Commissioner for the City of London 1863–90. Sir James, who had to cope with the murderous exploits of Jack the Ripper in London's East End, had earlier been responsible for establishing the first police force in Berkshire in 1856

30 A family affair. Deputy Chief
Constable John Reynolds, his son
Superintendent William Reynolds and
his grandson Pc William John
Reynolds, all members of
Hertfordshire police c.1905

Meeting trouble

31   Men of Bristol Police Force performing cutlass drill in
1877. Although these weapons were never issued as
standard equipment a supply was kept in most police
armouries for possible use during major disturbances.

'The police constable is to be given to understand distinctly
that the sword is put into his hand merely as a defensive
weapon in case his life should be in danger, and that he
shall not use or even draw it for any less weighty cause;
he will be called to strict account and will most probably
be dismissed.' (From a Metropolitan Police Order of 1832)

32 Great trouble was feared by the government when
20,000 Chartists descended on London on 10 April 1848
to present their famous six-point charter to Parliament.
Thousands of policemen and soldiers were armed and
placed on alert under the command of the Duke of
Wellington. Fortunately, events passed off peacefully, as
this record of the rally on Kennington Common shows. The
photograph is one of two daguerrotypes taken by Mr W.G.
Kilburn and was discovered recently among the Royal
Collection at Windsor. Not only the world's first
photograph of a protest rally, it is probably the first crowd
photograph as well

33 More than a hint of Victorian
melodrama in this photograph from
an early City of London Police manual
on unarmed combat, produced in
the early 1900s

34 (*left*) A rooftop protest during evictions at County Durham in 1891

35 (*below*) Handcuffed prisoners being marched from court at Watford, Hertfordshire, in 1902 after a riot which earned the town some unique and unflattering headlines during the crisis of King Edward VII's illness and the postponement of his coronation. When the local Coronation Committee – like those in every other community – cancelled the planned festivities, several hundred 'hooligans' went on the rampage attacking shops and property belonging to the committee members. More than 50 men and women were later fined or imprisoned

COLLIERY OFFICIALS &
WEST RIDING AND CHESHIRE CONSTABULARIES
At Wharncliffe Silkstone Colliery, South Yorkshire.

36 (*above, left*) Manchester policemen demonstrating their new Gladstone riot shields in a city park in 1913

37 (*left*) Winston Churchill, then Home Secretary, visiting the scene of the siege of Sidney Street in London's East End, during January 1911

38 (*above*) During the Great Coal Strike of 1893 pits in Yorkshire, Lancashire and the Midlands were closed for more than four months. The miners were protesting at an attempt by the coal owners to reduce wages by 20 per cent and the dispute was settled only after government intervention. The photograph shows men of the West Riding and Cheshire constabularies with officials of the Wharncliffe Silkstone Colliery in South Yorkshire

39 1893 was a year of extensive industrial strife. Policemen from Hull, Leeds, York, Huddersfield and the East Riding, together with a few wives, aboard R.M.S. *Eldorado* which was converted into a temporary police station during a strike by dockers at Hull

40 A formidable escort for a very small demonstration by suffragettes in Manchester, 1909

41   If these 'special constables' – recruited during a
parliamentary election at Whitby, Yorkshire, in 1864 –
appear more capable of breaking the law than upholding it,
there is a story which explains it all. Most *were* local
trouble-makers who became victims of a ruse by the local
police superintendent for which they never forgave him.
On the day of the election he put out word that he was
expecting trouble from outside and needed volunteers to
help the police. Relishing the prospect of a good punch-up
on the side of the law for a change the lads sped round to
the station which they were sworn in and issued with
arm bands and truncheons. They were then placed inside
the building where they were told they were on 'emergency
stand-by'. By various expedients such as drills and having
their photograph taken they were kept occupied until the
election excitement had died down. When all was quiet
the superintendent solemnly thanked and dismissed them.
Only when they were outside did the penny drop!

Prison life

42 A Victorian Black Maria discharging a group of
prisoners at Wormwood Scrubs, London, *c.*1890. These
were probably 'local' prisoners, that's to say those
sentenced to two years or less who would serve their time
in a prison in their home area

43 The policemen who delivered the prisoners to gaol had to obtain a certificate as proof that all had been delivered safely

44 Making out the record card – weight, height, trade, religion, next-of-kin. From this moment until the end of his sentence the prisoner lost his identity and was addressed only by his number

45 A convict detained under the Separate System, working, eating and sleeping alone in his cell.

'As a general rule, a few months in the separate cell render a prisoner strangely impressible. The chaplain can then make the brawn navvy cry like a child; he can work his feeling in any way he pleases; he can, so to speak, photograph his own thoughts, wishes and opinions on his patient's mind, and fill his mouth with his own phrases and language.' (The Rev John Clay, Chaplain at Preston Gaol, 1861)

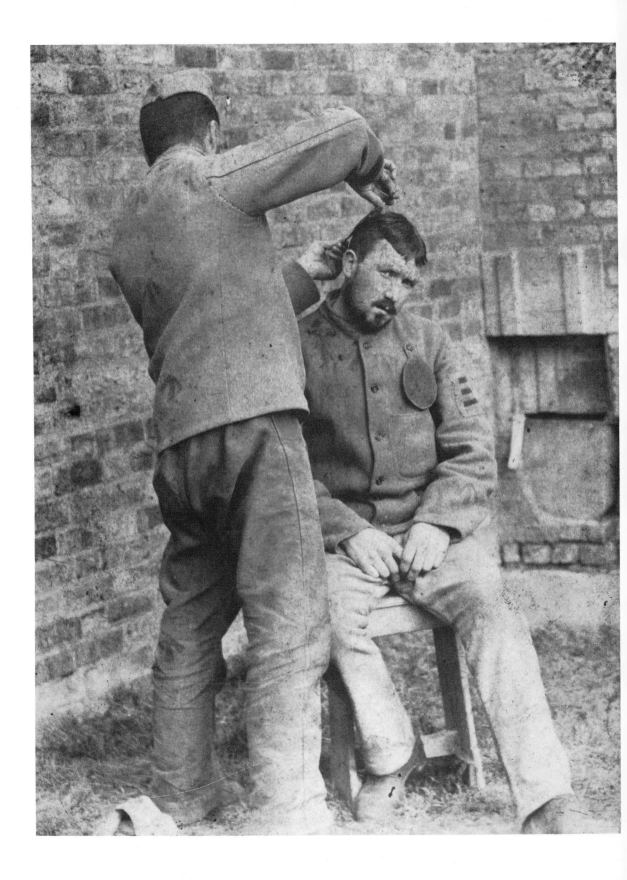

46 (*left*) The first prison haircut at Wormwood Scrubs. Only convicts sentenced to penal servitude had their heads shaved – the hair was allowed to grow again three months before release

47 A prison warder outside a cell in Gloucester gaol *c*.1900. The plaque by the door would have held the prisoner's record card

48 The bakehouse at Wormwood Scrubs *c.*1890. The master baker was a member of the staff, his assistants all prisoners. In late Victorian times the bakehouse turned out some 5,000 small loaves each day for the 1,400 inmates

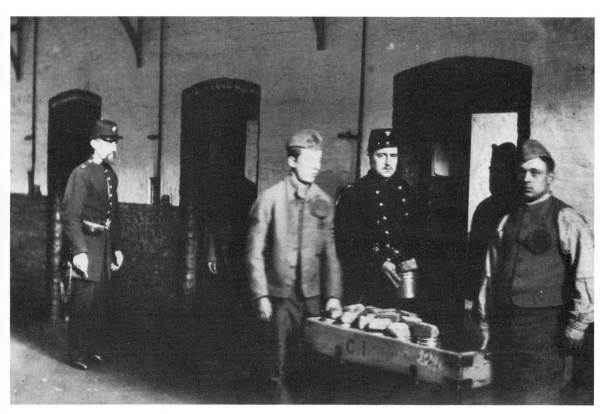

49 Dinner being delivered to prisoners in separate cells. By the end of the nineteenth century prison food was of such a high standard that – for hundreds of undernourished men and women from the slum areas – a spell in gaol became a positive pleasure. The following poem was reputedly found carved on a piece of slate at Portland Convict Prison:

I cannot take my walks abroad, I'm under lock and key
And much the public I applaud for their kind care of me.
Not more than others I deserve, in fact much less than more
Yet I have bread while others starve and beg from door to door.
The honest pauper in the street half-naked I behold
Whilst I am clad from head to foot and covered from the cold.
Thousands there are who scarce can tell where they may lay their head.
But I've a warm and well-aired cell, a bath, good books, a bed.
Whilst they are fed on workhouse fare and grudged their scanty food
Three times a day my meals I get, sufficient, wholesome, good.
Then to the British Public's health, who all our cares relieve
And while they treat us as they do, they'll never want for thieves.

50 (*above, left*) A basket-weaving class at Dartmoor, 1893. Convicts unfit for hard labour were taught a light trade by a qualified instructor

51 (*left*) The Dartmoor twine walk. Much of the country's twine and string was made in Britain's Victorian prisons

52 (*above*) Bundles of firewood provided a small source of income for Gloucester gaol at the turn of the century

53 Laying paving stones at
Gloucester gaol *c*.1900

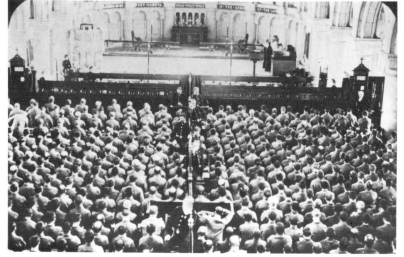

54 (*above*) Dartmoor prison stores in about 1893

55 (*left*) Sunday service in the Protestant chapel, Wormwood Scrubs 1893

57 (*right*) Prisoners at Gloucester on a practice turn-out with an early manual fire-fighting pump

58 (*below, right*) Sir Joshua Jebb (1793–1863), first surveyor-general of convict prisons. Portland, Chatham, Dartmoor and Portsmouth prisons were designed largely by him

59   William Watkins, a warder at
Gloucester gaol at the turn of the
century

Women and children

60   Mrs Emmeline Pankhurst (1858–1928) under arrest
during the suffragettes' attack on Buckingham Palace in
May 1914. In all 66 women were arrested when they tried
to storm a police cordon in order to present a petition to
King George V

61 Women prison officers at
Wormwood Scrubs in the 1890s, when
the prison had a women's wing

62 The hardest work performed by women prisoners at The Scrubs was in the laundry, which dealt with the clothing and linen for the entire prison population of some 1,400

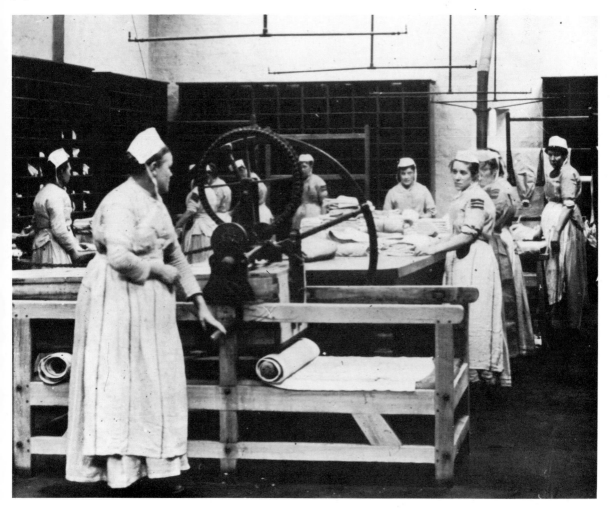

64 Boys aged 11 and 13 who, in 1899, were sentenced to five days' hard labour in Portsmouth prison for wilfully damaging a door by throwing mortar at it

63 Tending a modest flower garden at Gloucester gaol *c*.1900

6th Janry 18 77

PARTICULARS of a Person convicted of a Crime specified in the 20th Section of
the Prevention of Crimes Act, 1871.

Name .... *Dennis Fairey*

and

Aliases ....

Age (on discharge) .... *9 years*	Photograph of Prisoner.
Height .... *3 ft 9*	
Hair .... *D^k Brown*	
Eyes .... *Blue*	
Complexion .... *Pale*	
Where born .... *Ellington Hunts*	
Married or single .... *Single*	
Trade or occupation .... *School Boy*	
Any other distinguishing mark ...... *None*	

Description when liberated.

Address at time of apprehension............ *Huntingdon*

Whether summarily disposed of or tried by
a Jury. *Summarily*

Place and date of conviction .... *Huntingdon 19th Decr 1876.*

Offence for which convicted................. *Stealing a loaf of bread and
a Quantity of oranges apples and nuts.*

HUN'

PARTICULARS of Persons convicted of
Criminals' Act, 1869, and who w
date hereof, either on expiration

Name................. .... *Ju*

and

Aliases .... *o*

Age (on discharge)	
Height......................	
Hair........................	
Eyes........................	
Complexion	
Where born	
Married or single	
Trade or occupation	
Any other distinguishing mark..	

Description when liberated.

Address at time of apprehension...

Whether summarily disposed of or
by a Jury.

Place and date of conviction ....

Offence for which convicted ......

---

65 In Christmas Week of 1876 this little boy was caught
stealing a loaf and a small quantity of fruit and nuts.
Dennis, who was only nine years old, was sentenced to
21 days' hard labour followed by four years in a
reformatory. Like the other children here he had no
previous convictions, but because of the prison sentence
he had to take his place among the 'habitual criminals' in
the record book of Huntingdon County Gaol

66 For stealing a loaf in
Grantham in 1872, Julia, aged
11, was sentenced to 14 days in
prison followed by five years
in a reformatory

OUNTY GAOL,

5ᵗʰ January 18 72

d in the First Schedule of Habitual
m this Gaol within seven days from
a Licence from Secretary of State.

othorpe

Photograph of Prisoner.

ham

mmarily

ingdon 27 Janᵞ 1872

ing Bread

HUNTINGDON COUNTY GAOL,

6ᵗʰ Novʳ 1875

Particulars of a Person convicted of a Crime specified in the 20th Section of the Prevention of Crimes Act, 1871.

Name .... Samuel Hayes

and

Aliases ....

Description when liberated.

Age (on discharge) 12

Height .... 4 feet 7¾

Hair .... Dᵏ Brown

Eyes .... Hazel

Complexion .... Fresh

Where born .... Grantham

Married or single .... Single

Trade or occupation .... Labourer

Any other distinguishing mark .... Yes

Small scar from burn on lower part of right thumb also small scar on forehead from dog bite.

Address at time of apprehension .... Peterborough

Whether summarily disposed of or tried by a Jury. .... Summarily

Place and date of conviction .... Norman Cross 3ʳᵈ Novʳ 1875

Offence for which convicted .... Stealing three doz Brass Window Blind fittings.

Photograph of Prisoner.

67 Samuel, aged 12 years and described in the record book as 'a labourer', received a short sharp sentence for stealing window-blind fittings in 1875 – 14 days' hard labour and nine strokes with the birch rod

68 A fencing class for delinquent
boys on the Wellesley Nautical
Training Ship

69 Lost children who found
themselves with rather overwhelming
police protection during a Wimbledon
Rifle Meeting in South London, in
1867

70 (*above*) Shortly after Police Sergeant Robert Bentley was murdered by anarchists in the incident that led to the Siege of Sidney Street his widow gave birth to their second child. Many of the hero's colleagues from the City of London Police were at the baby's christening in 1911

71 (*right*) Young ragamuffin in trouble on Brighton sea-front in the early 1900s

72 (*left*) Friendly advice for a law-abiding toddler in Tottenham, North London, *c*.1906

73 (*above*) Well before the days of the 'lollipop man', an Edwardian policeman on school patrol in City Road, Manchester

74 (*below*) A case being heard at a Birmingham juvenile court in 1905. The young defendant sits in the foreground with his back to the camera

Buildings

75 The entrance to Wormwood Scrubs Prison, West London, *c*.1894 – built entirely by convict labour. The wall medallions depict the prison reformers Elizabeth Fry and John Howard

76 Scotland Yard police headquarters began life in the house on the left of this photograph, taking its name from the courtyard which was a part of the Palace of Westminster once set aside for use by visiting Scottish monarchs. The central building was the Public Carriage Office, where owners of London's hackney carriages obtained their licences

77 Godalming police station, Surrey, decorated for the Diamond Jubilee celebrations in 1897. A typical example of the small-town police stations built in late Victorian times combining the station office with living accommodation

78 (*right*) The old town gaol at Cambridge stood in Gonville Place from 1827–78. It was one of many small prisons demolished when the government assumed control of all prisons being run by the local authorities

79 (*below*) The House of Correction at Devizes, Wiltshire, was designed as a 16-sided polygon with the governor's office in a central circular building from which he could observe all 16 cell blocks and exercise yards. In 1911 the prison closed and, after temporary use as a military detention centre during the First World War, was eventually demolished to make way for a housing estate

80　The site in Wapping High Street where the Thames Police Force was founded in 1797; it is now the divisional headquarters. The 'new' building, opened in 1869, has since been much extended. Photograph c.1900 (see also plates 98–103)

81　The men's cell block at Lawford's Gate House of Correction, Bristol, in 1907. The prison was built to replace the city's old gaol, destroyed by fire during the Bristol Riots of 1831. It was acquired by Bristol Corporation in 1906 and demolished in 1923 when the land was needed for housing

82 Holloway Women's Prison in North London *c.*1890, showing discharged prisoners being met by friends and relatives

83 Pc Horn of the Devon Constabulary outside his picturesque police cottage in Rock Walk, Torquay in 1905

84 (*above*) Newgate prison, London, *c*.1895. The gaol was demolished in 1902 and five years later King Edward VII came to this spot in Holborn to open the new building that had risen on the site, the Old Bailey Central Criminal Court

85 (*left*) The old village lock-up at Kilmersdon, near Bath. A feature of most rural communities, the lock-up was a convenient place to detain local drunks and vagrants. Conditions inside were primitive – a wooden bed, straw on the floor and a bucket in the corner

Dartmoor
and hard labour

86 A convict working party at the entrance to Princetown Prison, Dartmoor. Carved on the granite archway the Latin inscription *Parcere Subjectis* – Spare the Suppressed. The photograph, like the remainder in this chapter, was taken in the early 1890s

87 (*above*) Because many convicts worked outside the prison walls, prison officers were armed with breach-loader rifles. The 'warder-sentries', as they were then known, had orders to shoot a man who refused to halt while trying to escape

88 (*right*) One of several stations built at strategic points across Dartmoor. Each one was within sight of two others and each had a small tower from which semaphore or light signals could be sent in the event of an attempted escape. The men in the foreground are cleaning tools used for stone dressing

89 One of the toughest forms of work on Dartmoor, land reclamation. In late-Victorian times some 20 acres of the moor was cleared and drained for agricultural use each year

90 The stone quarry, scene of the most trying of all convict labours where men only of first-class physical fitness were put to work

91 Splitting and dressing the quarried granite for building purposes

92 In bitter weather working parties took with them light-weight windbreaks to protect them from the biting winds during rest periods. At the feet of the warder-sentry is an urn which would have contained either tea or soup

93 Breaking granite for road construction and repairs. Each convict is wearing goggles to protect his eyes from flying stone splinters

94 Harrowing a field on the prison farm – surely the only farm in England where harrows were pulled not by horses but by human beings

95 (*left*) A new cell block under construction. Most of the prison was built by convict labour and a good many men returned to society to become fully-qualified master masons

96 (*below*) Grooming livestock in the prison farmyard. The bull apparently was 'a dangerous customer who respected nobody but the prisoner beside him'

97 With so much moorland pasture available, large numbers of sheep were reared at the prison. The ram in the foreground was a particularly fine specimen which won several prizes in agricultural shows – prizes which went not to the convicts but to the 'owner' of Her Majesty's Prison at Princetown, Queen Victoria

Policemen afloat
and fighting fires

98   Coxwain Robert Miller and Sub-Inspector Thomas
Garland of the London River Police at the helm of the
steam launch *Watch*.
Photograph *c*.1900

99 Marine police patrolled the River Thames by rowing galley for more than 100 years. The original force was established by shipping merchants in 1798 at a time when importers were losing £500,000 a year through thefts from ships and warehouses

100 A former Royal Navy survey ship, H.M.S. *Royalist* was one of two floating hulks used as river police stations throughout much of the last century. This hulk, photographed during low tide at Blackwall in 1884, also served as the home of the station inspector and his family

101 Taking a sample off Wapping Creek in 1900. London River Police had to make regular checks for excessive water pollution caused by factories and homes discharging effluent into the Thames

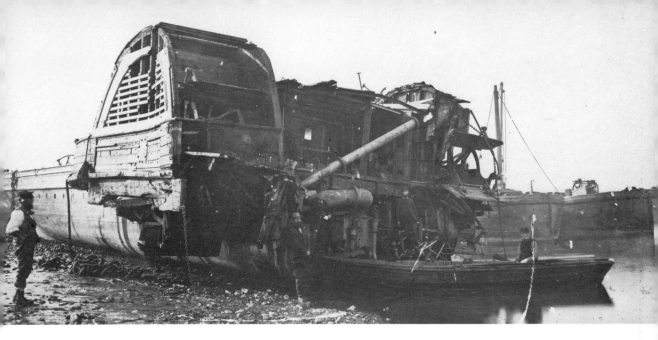

102 The aftermath of the worst sailing disaster in the history of the Thames. In 1878 the paddle steamer *Princess Alice*, on a pleasure trip, was in collision with a collier and sank with the loss of 600 lives

103 Largely because of difficulties experienced by the police in coping with the *Princess Alice* disaster pressure was put on the authorities to supply the force with powered craft and, in 1884, two steam launches were purchased

104 The horse-drawn 'steamer' used by York Police Fire Brigade in 1907. The horses were trained to respond to the alarm bell by trotting from their stable to positions beneath a special harness which was suspended from the ceiling. This could be lowered onto them and clipped secure in a matter of seconds

106 A novel machine used by men of the Salford brigade in 1890. A set of three tandem bicycles and a tandem trike enabled the police-firemen to tow their ladder and hose cart by pedal power

105 The steam pump of South Shields Police Fire Brigade undergoing tests in 1898. These machines were coal-fired and remained in use until well into the present century. At particularly big fires supplies of coal had to be delivered to the scene to ensure that the steamers kept up sufficient pressure to pump water for the hoses

107   Firemen turncocks of the
Liverpool Police Fire Brigade in 1879

Tasks and punishments

108 Penance in the stocks outside Redruth Police Station, Cornwall, *c.*1860. This centuries-old punishment for drunks, rowdies and other minor miscreants was never officially abolished but died out in the second half of the nineteenth century. The last recorded case was at Rugby in 1865

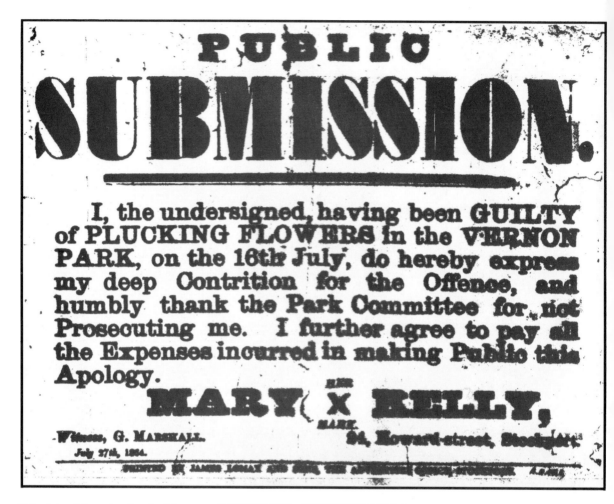

PUBLIC SUBMISSION.

I, the undersigned, having been GUILTY of PLUCKING FLOWERS in the VERNON PARK, on the 16th July, do hereby express my deep Contrition for the Offence, and humbly thank the Park Committee for not Prosecuting me. I further agree to pay all the Expenses incurred in making Public this Apology.

MARY (X) KELLY,

HER MARK.

Witness, G. MARSHALL.
July 27th, 1864.

94, Howard-street, Stockport.

109 (*above*) Some local authorities allowed minor offenders to avoid prosecution by making a public apology on wall posters pasted up in the vicinity – as happened to Mary Kelly when she was caught picking flowers in a park in Stockport

110 (*right*) The chain room at Dartmoor, showing 'the triangle' to which prisoners were strapped for flogging. The heavy leg irons below were used only for the most violent convicts while the curbing chains and handcuffs were used if groups of convicts had to be transported long distances

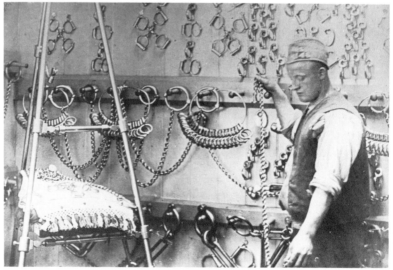

111 The treadwheel at York Castle prison, showing part of the mechanism which enabled the wheel to power a circular saw – used to cut up wood for the prison's fires. The photograph, with a warder and two visitors acting as models, was taken in 1907 shortly before the wheel was dismantled and sold to Madame Tussaud's museum

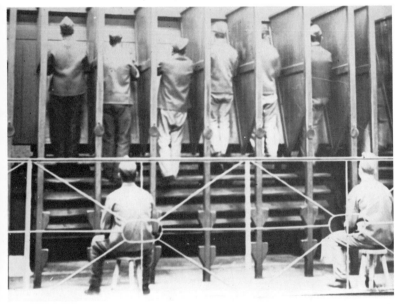

112 The treadwheel at Pentonville Prison in London *c*.1890 – showing two prisoners enjoying the five-minute rest which was allowed every 15 minutes. 'At nine o'clock we were marched off to the Weel room. It was like walking up steps and never getting any higher, but verry hard work and we was kept at it from nine to twelve. Then came dinner. . . . We were put on the Weel again from one o'clock till four in the afternoon, then we were set to pick okum till eight, wen we went to bed'. (An extract from a letter written in 1870 by a boy of 14 while serving a month's hard labour in Norwich gaol for poaching)

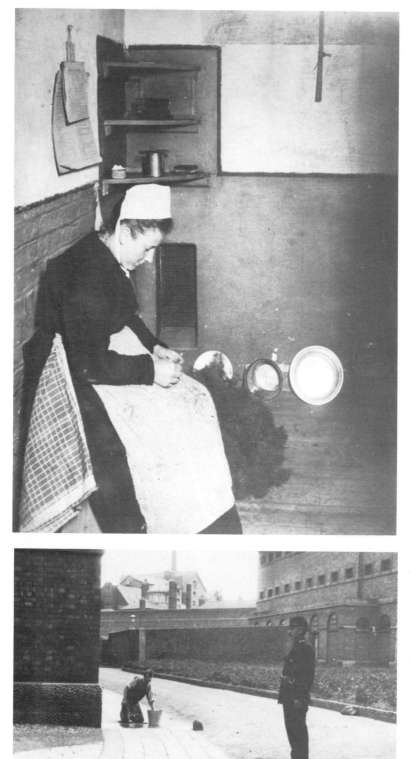

113 Picking oakum was a task performed in prisons and workhouses throughout Victorian times. The work involved untwisting and teasing out lengths of old tarred rope, which made inexperienced fingers raw and painful. The oakum was used for caulking the seams of wooden ships and boats. A photograph taken in Wormwood Scrubs women's wing *c.*1893

114 (*left*) Scrubbing the pavement at Gloucester gaol *c.*1900

115 (*right*) The crank at Wormwood Scrubs was set at 12-lb pressure and during his first month of hard labour a prisoner had to complete 10,000 revolutions a day. Both the crank and the treadwheel were eventually banned by act of Parliament in 1898

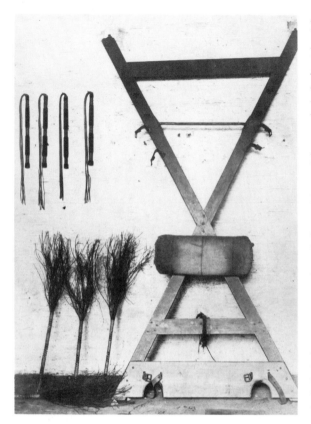

Strapped to a post hands in the air,
The very picture of blank despair.
A prisoner is going to receive a birching.
The doctor and governor with faces grim
Stand there quietly watching him
Receive his awful punishment.
His flesh is naked from head to hips,
A warder, a birch in his hand grips,
Waiting the governor's order.

He reads the sentence, waves his hand
The Chief Warder give the command
'Do your duty, show no quarter'
Stroke by stroke, bit by bit
The wails come out as he is hit
With the birch by a stalwart warder.
And as the terrible pain he feels
For mercy then he loudly yells.
With convulsed face he looks around –
No mercy is there to be found
Until the last stroke is finished.

On the wounds they put vaseline and lint
Then from the post he is unbent.
They give him a drink of water.
Ill and faint, his strength all spent
In pain his folly he would repent.
For some time he feels the pain
And vows he would never offend again.
For the future he will be content
To quietly serve his time.

116 Equipment used for administering corporal punishment at Wormwood Scrubs in the 1890s. The poem was written by a man from that prison after he had received a birching ordered upon him by a visiting magistrate:

Coping with traffic

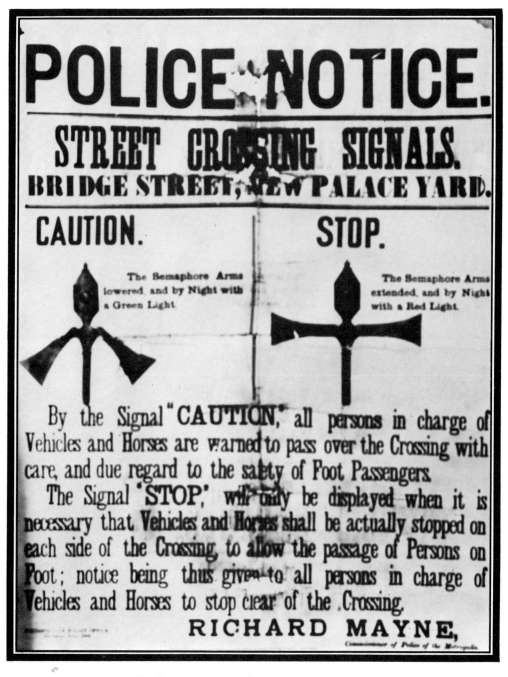

117 The world's first automatic traffic signals were tried out on the London public in 1868. They consisted of semaphore arms which extended to give pedestrians precedence over horse-drawn vehicles at a particularly busy junction in Westminster. The test ended abruptly one night when the gas-lit equipment blew up and it was 50 years before the idea was tried out again – this time using electricity

118 (*above*) A lone policeman
(foreground, left) endeavouring to
unravel a mix-up of tram cars and
goods carts at the junction of Mosley
Street and York Street, Manchester
c.1905

119 (*right*) A City of London policeman
controlling traffic in 1873. Traffic
congestion was common in London
and other big cities long before the
arrival of the motor car. In 1829
Metropolitan policemen were
reporting seasonal traffic jams
involving horse-drawn vehicles which
sometimes took an hour to sort out

120 A dead horse and a car in a
ditch on the A39 near Wadebridge,
Cornwall in 1910. Such incidents
occurred all too frequently during the
first decade of this century when
people, animals and roads were totally
unprepared for the power and speed
of the motor car

121 Transporting a road casualty by hand ambulance in Piccadilly in 1910. Hand ambulances were used between 1860 and 1938 – not only for casualties but also for restraining drunks and violent suspects who could be strapped firmly in and carted off to the police station

122 A Huntingdonshire police cyclist *c*.1890. Many forces issued their men with bicycles not simply for transport but to catch 'scorchers' – groups of speeding cyclists. Some Chief Constables considered this work sufficiently hazardous to justify paying their men an extra *3d* a day danger money

123 Edwardian policemen experimented with numerous ways of trapping speeding motorists. One was to time the vehicle over a measured distance, which involved one officer concealing himself on a roof and signalling to his colleague with the stop watch at the other end

124 (*above*) A crossroads encounter at St Albans, Hertfordshire, in 1912 which resulted in each driver being fined £5 for careless driving

125 (*left*) Two men were killed and many injured when this Birmingham Corporation tram crashed in Carver Street after a brakes failure in October 1907. The accident was one of several that occurred during the early days of the city's tramway system

126 An accident on Newport Bridge
*c.*1910

127   The Aerial Navigation Act of
1913 banned low flying over military
installations, to prevent aerial espionage.
The same year the pilot of this
Nieuport Water Plane was arrested
when he landed on the Thames at
Blackwall after inadvertently flying
low over Woolwich Arsenal. The
magistrate gave him a conditional
discharge

Murder!

128 The arrest of the Essex murderer Samuel Dougal who was executed in July 1903 after shooting Camille Holland, a wealthy spinster with whom he had lived at Moat Farm, Clavering. He buried the body on the estate and the murder, committed in 1899, came to light only several years later after he was caught forging cheques in the dead woman's name. Dougal denied the murder until his last moments on the scaffold at Springfield Gaol, Chelmsford. Then, as the executioner went to pull the lever, the prison chaplain called out 'Guilty or Not Guilty Dougal?' From behind the white hood came Dougal's last word before dying – 'Guilty'

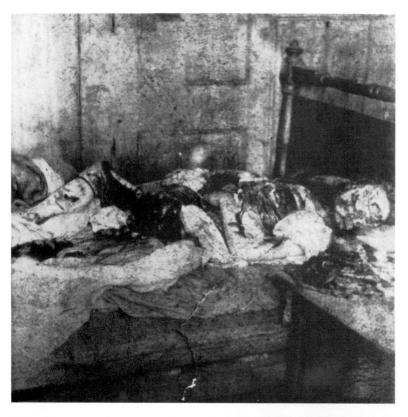

129 Jack the Ripper's fifth and most horrific murder. The dismembered body of the prostitute Mary Jane Kelly, aged 24, as it was found in a room at Millers Court, Whitechapel, in November 1888

130 The remains of the murdered actress Belle Elmore, better known as Mrs Cora Crippen, as found under the cellar of her home in Hilldrop Crescent, Islington, London, in 1910

132 (*left*) Crippen being brought back to England after trying to escape to America with his mistress Ethel Le Neve aboard the S.S. *Montrose*. The liner's captain became suspicious of the couple (who were disguised as father and son) and sent a radiogram alerting Scotland Yard. The police overtook the *Montrose* in a faster vessel and made the arrests

133 (*below, left*) A photograph – taken secretly with a concealed camera – showing Crippen and his mistress in the dock at Bow Street. He was hanged in November 1910. Ethel Le Neve was found not guilty and set free. She managed to reclaim anonymity and later married. She died at Dulwich, South London, in 1967 at the age of 84

134 (*below*) The scaffold and 'drop' at York Castle prison – used for county executions until the turn of the century

135 William Calcraft (1800–1879) best-known of the Victorian hangmen. He began his career at Newgate prison where he was paid 10s 0d a week for flogging juvenile offenders. He succeeded John Foxton as hangman in 1829 and performed the last public execution outside Newgate on 26 May 1868. A cobbler by trade he was reputed to be a kindly man who was very fond of children and animals

136   Manchester policemen outside Strangeways prison at the time of an execution in the 1890s

137 William Murphy – the last man
to be hanged in Caernarvon county
gaol – photographed at Beaumaris
prison, Anglesey, where he gave
himself up after murdering a woman
friend, Gwen Ellen Jones, on Christmas
Day 1909. He was executed the
following February

Parades, celebrations and moments off-duty

138 The staff of Taunton police station, Somerset, celebrating Queen Victoria's Golden Jubilee in 1887

139 The pioneer members of Manchester City Police Band, formed in the 1880s when the well-trimmed moustache was clearly very fashionable

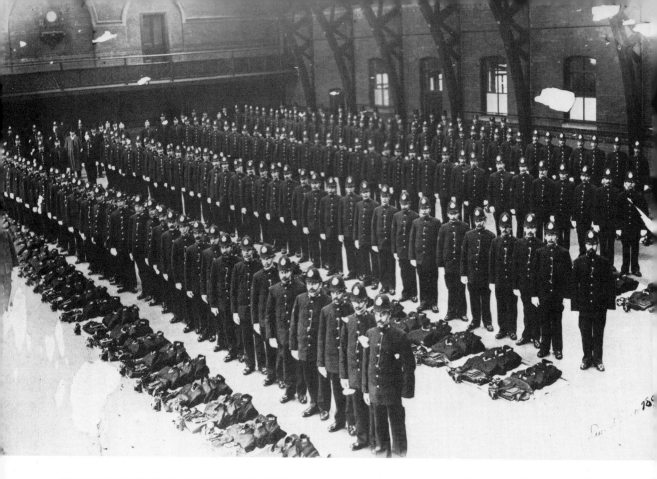

140 (*above*) Some 150 Bradford City policemen on inspection during the Diamond Jubilee celebrations of 1897

141 (*left*) An escort of straw-helmets for the by-election winner Cecil Harmsworth M.P. at Luton, Bedfordshire, in 1911. These police helmets, worn for coolness in the summer, reflected the straw hat industry for which Luton became famous

142 A quiet moment for some of the
Glamorgan Constabulary who were
drafted to St Austell, Cornwall, in 1913
to help deal with disorders caused
by the clay pit strikes

143 A reminder of the days when a landlord offered a churchwarden pipe for customers to smoke with their ale

144 Sergeant-Major Piddick teaching quarter-staff drill to the daughters of Mr Gerald de Courcey Hamilton, Chief Constable of Devon, *c.*1870

145 An assortment of characters on the fishquay at North Shields c.1880, including a policeman wearing the 'new' uniform supplied to the local force in 1878

146 Fancy dress competitors at Exeter Police Sports in 1909

147 A dozen heavyweights who made up the formidable tug-o-war team of Bristol City Police in 1906